12/16

W9-DHW-537

JEWELRY
for Your Table

LISA GUERRERO

Photography by
WENDY KATHLEEN MCELFISH
& WALTER COLES

Schiffer
Publishing Ltd

4880 Lower Valley Road • Atglen, PA 19310

Designed by *Danielle D. Farmer*
Cover design by *Danielle D. Farmer*
Type set in Goudy Old Style

ISBN: 978-0-7643-5249-2
Printed in China

Published by Schiffer Publishing, Ltd.
4880 Lower Valley Road
Atglen, PA 19310
Phone: (610) 593-1777; Fax: (610) 593-2002
E-mail: Info@schifferbooks.com
Web: www.schifferbooks.com

For our complete selection of fine books on this and related subjects, please visit our website at www.schifferbooks.com. You may also write for a free catalog.

Schiffer Publishing's titles are available at special discounts for bulk purchases for sales promotions or premiums. Special editions, including personalized covers, corporate imprints, and excerpts, can be created in large quantities for special needs. For more information, contact the publisher.

We are always looking for people to write books on new and related subjects. If you have an idea for a book, please contact us at proposals@schifferbooks.com.

In memory of my mother, Lucy,
1943–1973

The *Soul* of an Artist, The *Spirit* of a Warrior

Contents

For more than twenty years, I've traveled the
nation as a TV journalist.

It's

been said I have a split personality and I've got to admit,
it's true. And that's a good thing because the person I
am during my "day job" as an investigative reporter,
chasing down bad guys and shouting tough questions,
wouldn't be as pleasant to be around every evening as my
"alter-ego," a laid-back artist with a craft project in one
hand and a glass of wine in the other.

Thankfully, I've learned through trial and error to
live a life of fulfillment and balance where I can be
both strong and assertive at work yet creative and
artistic at home.

Here's a little bit about me and how I was inspired
to write *Jewelry for Your Table*.

For over twenty years I've been traveling around the
country as a national TV journalist—first as a sportscaster,
then as an entertainment reporter and currently as the
Chief Investigative Correspondent for *Inside Edition*.

My job requires long hours and a grueling schedule
that includes being on the road for days, even weeks at a
time, covering challenging and occasionally dangerous
assignments. My crew and I were once chased out of an
illegal cock-fighting operation by a band of angry men
with shotguns, and a few years ago I was hit by a car when
a dentist, accused of abusing his young patients, didn't

As a TV reporter, my days are busy and my schedule can be grueling.

like my hard-hitting questions. He gunned his sedan right into me and I'm proud to say that, although I ended up a bit battered and bruised, I didn't drop my microphone!

> My artwork helps me maintain a sense of peace and balance in my otherwise crazy life.

When my friends ask me how I've been able to sustain such a crazy schedule under difficult circumstances for over two decades, yet still appear relaxed, confident, and centered on camera, my answer is . . . BALANCE!

In addition to my job as a reporter, I've developed a second career as a mixed media artist. Over the years I've taken my love of arts and crafts to a deeper level by studying the process of building mosaics for the home. This has been a peaceful, relaxing, and creative process that recharges my batteries and brings artistic fulfillment to my life.

In a practical sense, creating art has been a meditative, calming counterpoint to the stressful and hectic shooting schedule that I'm required to maintain. The fact that I've worked in practically every state and in some incredibly interesting locations throughout the world has informed my art; I find inspiration everywhere I travel and I've collected pieces of vintage jewelry, baubles, and knickknacks during my assignments that I bring home to use in my projects.

My career as a reporter has made me a better artist and my art has made me a better journalist.

When I went on vacation in 2004, I fell in love with the colorful, intricate, ancient mosaics I discovered throughout Europe. When I returned to California I enrolled in a mosaic workshop to learn how to create designs, cut glass, ceramic and tile, and finally, how to grout and seal the pieces.

Once I learned the basics, I was off! I made everything from custom kitchen backsplashes to fireplace surrounds . . . even a huge, outdoor pizza oven!

My first large-scale wall hanging, *Malibu Mermaid* (24" × 36"), was accepted into exhibition at the Sebastopal Center for the Arts in Napa, California, and was published in *Best of Worldwide Mixed Media Artists*, Volume I (Kennedy Publishing). I was offered $10,000 for that piece but refused to sell her—I'm emotionally attached to my mermaid.

Inspired by ancient mosaics I saw in Europe, I began creating my own, working on everything from back-splashes to pizza ovens.

In 2009 I began a series of mosaics called *Backsplash Babes*, each one depicting women of different ethnicities embellished with actual kitchen utensils and "wearing" vintage costume jewelry. These were shown in art galleries in Beverly Hills and Santa Monica, leading to commissions from musicians, athletes, actors, and directors.

My mixed-media *Backsplash Babes* are in the kitchens of musicians, athletes and people from the film industry, including commissions by baseball's Johnny Damon and KISS guitarist Tommy Thayer.

Baseball superstar Johnny Damon purchased a *Backsplash Babe* called "Every Man's Dream" for his wife, Michelle, and KISS lead guitarist, Tommy Thayer, commissioned me to create a mosaic sign for his Mediterranean style home, Lago Villa.

Two of my favorite pieces are a kitchen backsplash and coordinating fireplace surround for the great room in a Spanish-style beach house in Malibu. I called the projects "Aztec Sunburst" and "Aztec Fire."

My work also includes home décor items such as embellished picture frames and stained-glass vases.

Recently, I began to develop smaller home décor pieces like stained-glass votives, vases, and embellished frames. These are all one-of-a-kind projects that can never be replicated because I hand-cut each piece of glass and ceramic before incorporating vintage jewelry into the mosaic. I don't sell these pieces; instead I give them as gifts. My friend, TV personality Jillian Barberie, has one of my favorite frames hanging in her home.

The common denominator for most of my home décor projects is the use of vintage jewelry. While waiting for just the right project to embellish with these treasures, I often wear the pieces myself. This way I feel even more connected to the jewelry and its unique history, making it that much more personal and meaningful to me when I give it a "second life" by incorporating it into a project. I prefer to use jewelry that has been worn or given to me by women in my family. These heirlooms are precious and make each piece of art priceless because of their personal connection to my heritage.

It is this collection of vintage and costume brooches and pendants that inspired me to create *Jewelry for Your Table*. I hope that you use this book as a source of inspiration to help you curate, create, and gift these beautiful pieces of art to those you love.

And I hope that through the artistic process you find harmony, peace, and balance in your life as well.

Enjoy!

Lisa Guerrero

01

DISCOVERING JEWELRY
for YOUR TABLE

A Passion Ignites

I AM A
sentimental FOOL

 s

I sit here handwriting this chapter in my journal, I am surrounded by a house full of keepsakes, mementos, pictures, and handmade crafts. The items that I gravitate to have a history. Sometimes that history is personal to me, connected through family, friends, or loved ones. But other items are a part of someone else's history, the stories and adventures unknown to me, but precious nevertheless.

I prefer old things—stuff with character, texture, and secrets. I also adore trinkets that sparkle, shine, and glimmer. I love color and craftsmanship and the tiny imperfections that naturally accompany age, experience, and a life well lived. Appreciating old things, handmade things, is in my blood. My grandpa Guerrero, once a tailor, became a wood craftsman late in life, and today at ninety-five, he still creates one-of-a-kind wooden bowls and keepsakes.

My first Christmas with the Guerrero side of the family. My mom is on the far left and I'm the little squirt sitting on my Aunt Sonia's knee.

My mother, Lucy, who died at the young age of twenty-nine from cancer, never had the pleasure of growing old. Lucy was an artist and craftswoman herself. As the daughter of a tailor, she sewed my clothes, created macramé plant hangers, and embroidered a huge needlepoint wall hanging of an enormous vase full of sunflowers for the childhood bedroom I shared with my baby brother Richard.

My love for handmade crafts is genetic. My grandpa Guerrero was a tailor and now makes beautiful wooden bowls, and my mother Lucy was an artist whose creations filled my childhood home.

Lucy was a beautiful, headstrong Chilean immigrant new to America when she met my father, Walter, a shy Southern boy from Kentucky with a slight drawl and a penchant for music, art, and photography. Lucy spoke broken English and Walter didn't speak any Spanish at all, but together they learned the language of love and soon they were married with two children.

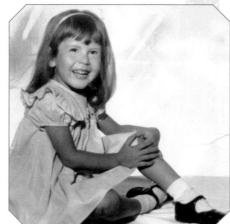

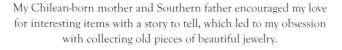

My Chilean-born mother and Southern father encouraged my love
for interesting items with a story to tell, which led to my obsession
with collecting old pieces of beautiful jewelry.

My dad became a social worker for The Salvation Army in San Diego and as a family, we spent countless hours in the basement of their building sifting through donated items—clothes, jewelry, knickknacks, and furniture. I learned early that one person's junk was another person's treasure. I saw baskets being filled with food and toys for families in need, and Christmas stockings being stuffed with gifts for us to take to the seniors at local nursing homes. At first the old people scared me until they held my hand and told me how thankful they were that we'd visited. Sometimes they'd want to tell stories, sing Christmas carols or pray, but mainly they just wanted a little bit of company and a kiss on the cheek.

As I got older, I became more and more interested in finding, collecting, and wearing items with a history. I would scour the thrift stores on Melrose Avenue in Los Angeles when I was a teenager, determined to find vintage clothes that would set me apart from the more popular "preppy" kids at my high school in Huntington Beach. Instead, I preferred the "rockabilly" style. I loved wearing dresses from the '50s, sweater sets, and especially the costume jewelry from that era.

My obsession with collecting old brooches, pendants, and earrings began there, sifting through dusty boxes of beat-up, broken jewelry, looking for only the special pieces that "spoke to me" and begged to be taken home, cleaned, repaired, and proudly worn.

Some of those vintage brooches that I collected during high school in the '80s are still in my studio to this day, and many are incorporated into my mixed-media art projects. I now have over a thousand pieces of jewelry in my studio, organized in boxes and cases by era, color, texture, size, theme, and value. But my jewelry doesn't live in those boxes exclusively.

I enjoy wearing my jewelry as often as I can, especially when I'm on camera reporting for *Inside Edition*, at a special event, or simply out to dinner.

Wearing vintage jewelry connects me with the women who wore the pieces before me.

Before I embellish a project with a brooch, pendant, or pair of chandelier earrings, I like to wear them first—to feel connected to the pieces and the mysterious women that wore these treasures before me.

Some of the jewelry in my collection were gifts from friends or passed down to me by family members. These items are especially precious and it used to make me a bit sad when, after wearing a piece, I would close it inside my jewelry box thinking it may be a long time until I see that beautiful treasure or family heirloom again.

This is how I discovered this gorgeous arts and crafts project by accident, and frankly, out of necessity.

One holiday season while planning to host a large Christmas dinner for extended family, I was excited to pull out my holiday china, crystal, silverware, and linens for this special occasion. A week before the party I was cleaning and arranging the place settings when I realized I didn't have any beautiful, Christmas-themed napkin rings. I had several perfectly pretty sets but nothing truly spectacular. Then I headed to a couple of department stores and a home décor boutique. I even searched online. Nothing.

This is the first *Jewelry for Your Table* napkin ring I created, using a Christmas pin my Grandma Coles left me.

I settled for a simple set of gold rings that I found in a drawer. I was walking by the mirror with my hands full of eight of those rings when I looked up and saw my reflection. I was wearing a hunter green sweater with a vintage Christmas brooch on my lapel. My Grandma Coles had left me the pin when she passed away years before, along with a cameo necklace and a simple set of pearls. As a Salvation Army officer, she was a woman who wore very little jewelry and no makeup at all. My dad's mother was a sweet, simple, and spiritual woman, so those few things she passed down to me are very precious indeed.

I stared at my image in the mirror and the enamel poinsettia set against a gold-toned base—the same gold color as the napkin rings I held in my hands. Something clicked!

Dropping the rings onto a table, I ran to my studio and pulled open the box marked "Vintage Christmas Pins." I pulled out seven of them that were approximately the same size with similar gold trim. I laid them out on the table next to the rings. Although each brooch was different—a Christmas tree, a snowflake, a stocking, a sleigh, reindeer, bells, etc.— they all complemented each other, being from the same era, and the gold trim matched the gold of the napkin rings.

Here are some of the original napkin rings I created out of both
necessity and serendipity, "Vintage Christmas."

After days of experimenting with jewelry, tools, techniques, and adhesives, I developed a process to clean, prepare, and build a set of "Vintage Christmas" napkin rings. I also discovered the best ways to "frame" these pieces of art with the right napkins, to tie the collection together with the china. When the table was finally set, my new creations glimmered, sparkled, and glowed in the candlelight. I thought to myself, "These napkin rings are like jewelry for my table!"

The project was a hit!

When my family sat down to dinner they immediately began raving about these pieces, examining all of the rings and passing them around the table so that everyone could admire the entire collection. My stepmom Pam called them "mini masterpieces," and as a crafter herself, wanted to learn the technique.

I posted pictures of my "Vintage Christmas" napkin rings on Facebook and Twitter. Immediately I was inundated with responses from women (and some men) asking for details. "How did you make them?" "Can you teach me?" "Would you be willing to sell those?"

I began to create and name dozens of napkin ring sets using my vintage brooch and pendant collection, each with a distinct theme: "Art Deco," "Gothic Crosses," "Cameo Appearance," "Medieval Medallions," "Blush Bouquet," "Tiny Dancers," etc. Every time I posted these online I received more encouraging responses. It was this wonderful feedback that inspired me to write this book.

> What could be more girly than a pair of ballerina napkin rings for a bridal shower or Mother's Day luncheon?

Most of us have a jewelry box in a closet, or a chest in an attic, filled with pieces of jewelry once meaningful but now tucked out of sight. You may have several items that are family heirlooms or inexpensive costume pieces that have some special significance but are stowed away in a drawer, all but forgotten and rarely worn, much less taken out, admired, and appreciated. I'll share my favorite collections with you to help fuel your imagination with the limitless possibilities of these one-of-a-kind "mini masterpieces." This book will teach you how to curate, create, and gift your own special sets of vintage jewelry embellished napkin rings.

Ralph Waldo Emerson once wrote, "Never lose an opportunity of seeing anything beautiful, for beauty is God's handwriting," and I encourage you not to lose an opportunity either.

Top left
I love to display my pins in acrylic jewelry boxes so they can be seen and admired.

It's time to open up these boxes, drawers, and treasure chests to learn another way to look at, admire, and share the beautiful things in your life by creating *Jewelry for Your Table*.

Top right
Even a simple, rustic pin makes an elegant table accessory.

02

BROOCHING *the* SUBJECT

The Power of Pins

WEAR YOUR *heart on* YOUR SLEEVE

*C*ostume

jewelry brooches or pins have long captured the fancy of ladies wanting to add sparkle to their ensemble or make a statement about their heritage, religion, politics, lover, or even their lack thereof!

Many of the projects in this book incorporate beautiful vintage brooches like this one. I actually had to replace two of the pearls on this piece, giving it an instant and inexpensive face lift (bottom right).

I remember being fourteen years old and watching the movie *Grease* with my best friend, Susie. In one scene, during a slumber party with "The Pink Ladies," Sandy gets her ear pierced by Frenchie with Marty's virgin pin. "Nice to know it's good for something," she quipped.

25

Susie and I almost dropped our popcorn. A virgin pin! A pin worn by virgins! Well, we certainly qualified so, inspired by the film, we made her mom take us to thrift stores to hunt for virgin pins both to wear and pierce our ears with.

Aaah, youth. Although I eventually outgrew the urge to prick my earlobes with sharp objects, I never stopped hunting through thrift stores to find amazing costume jewelry.

Most of the projects in this book feature beautiful, vintage brooches, although occasionally, I've incorporated large pendants onto the napkin rings, as I did for my set of "Gothic Crosses."

Because I'll be encouraging you to begin collecting these gorgeous pins, it's worth taking a look back to see why brooches have become such an important staple in our jewelry boxes . . . and our mothers', grandmothers' and great-grandmothers'.

Did you know that the brooch may have been the oldest type of jewelry ever worn? Found in caves from the Paleolithic Age were examples of pins made from thorns and flint that were likely used to hold pieces of animal skin together. Of course, back then they were used for practical rather than decorative purposes, but that began to change with the development of metals and fastening mechanisms.

Another interesting aspect of these early brooches is that they were worn by both men and women. Because their purpose was functional, everyone needed to use them. Later, what were once simply garment fasteners became ornamental, signifying the wearer's cultural or religious affiliation. Men in Ireland and Scotland from about AD 700–900, for example, wore Celtic brooches. An early Irish law even specified that sons of major kings

should have "brooches of gold" while sons of minor kings should wear silver brooches instead.

Throughout history, the style and designs of ornamental pins have changed with societal and fashion trends and sometimes signified an emotional attachment to a person or place. Medieval pilgrims wore brooches to signify a trip to a religious shrine. Pins with patron saints and carved cameos were worn in the sixteenth century. During the nineteenth century, lovers would wear a brooch with a lock of hair from their beloved, captured under glass. I find these sentimental examples of people almost literally wearing their "heart on their sleeve" to be incredibly sweet.

Since the early twentieth century, brooches have pretty much remained the domain of women, worn primarily as ornamentation and signifying cultural heritage, status, familial connection, or a personal style aesthetic. Here are some popular brooch trends through the years:

VICTORIAN

From approximately 1840 to 1900, these pin designs were sentimental: hearts, cameos, and flowers, often with pearls and semi-precious stones.

EDWARDIAN

Early twentieth century, these pieces were usually delicate and lacy, featuring rhinestones, pearls, and enamel.

ART NOUVEAU

From 1890 to 1910, these pins featured flowing, curved lines and colorful enamel.

ART DECO

From the 1920s through 1940s, these classic designs were bold and geometric, often featuring rhinestones.

NEW LOOK

Post World War II, these brooches had clean lines and often incorporated pearls or colored rhinestones.

MOD

These designs from the 1960s and 1970s featured lots of primary colored flowers as well as earth-toned ethnic designs.

NEW WAVE

These pins from the late 1970s through the 1980s tend to be brightly colored—even neon, in bold shapes, and slightly larger in size than other brooches.

Throughout history many celebrities, politicians, and fashion icons have worn brooches. Recently, Princess Kate, Selma Hayek, Michelle Obama, and Emma Stone have all been photographed wearing these ladylike accessories. When journalist Maria Bartiromo wore a large, vintage brooch while moderating a presidential debate, social media went wild, declaring #BroochesAreBack. The greatest newsmaker to be associated with wearing pins is one of the most influential women in American history, Madeleine Albright, the first female secretary of state and the author of a book about her brooch collection, *Read My Pins: Stories from a Diplomat's Jewel Box.*

Secretary Albright's personal relationship with brooches wasn't simply about ornamentation; it was also about diplomacy. Here is how she explains it:

My long and complicated interactions with Saddam Hussein yielded — surprisingly — a fashion moment that has continued to impact my career in diplomacy. In 1994, Hussein called me, the only woman involved in the diplomatic process in the Middle East at that time, a snake. Determined not to back down, I wore a snake pin the next day. From then on, I wore pins for different occasions — a dove pin for peace negotiations, or one my daughter made me as a toddler for Valentine's Day each year. Every day I wear a pin now, and every day it reflects a message.

Of course, the easiest way to wear a pin is on the right or left lapel of a solid colored blazer or over the bust of a simple dress. But these days, many women are updating the traditional look of a brooch with a more modern take. I love the idea of mixing vintage-looking jewelry with modern trends. For example, I regularly put a cameo brooch on the lapel of my leather jacket or an art deco pin on my denim shirt. Another fun way to use pins in an unexpected place is to embellish a straw hat with a mid-century modern floral brooch or attach a rhinestone pin to the front of a small clutch evening bag. Do you love scarves? Then use a brooch to secure it to your shoulder — I appreciate the practical aspect of doing this, especially in nasty, windy weather! Speaking of that, have you thought of embellishing your gloves or mittens with a crystal pin on one wrist? This is a gorgeous look, especially at night. I am such a fan of wearing my brooches in unusual ways that I have even attached a turquoise pin to the top of my brown suede cowboy boots and pinned a trio of rhinestone butterfly pins into a braid of my hair!

Give traditional brooches a modern twist by wearing them in unexpected ways, like on a glove, hat, or boot, or as a hair accessory.

There are other ways to add sparkle to your home using costume jewelry before you embellish a napkin ring with it. I love to take chandelier earrings and press them into pillar candles or slip a costume jewelry ring over tapered candles as a way of dressing up a table setting.

Brooches add additional sparkle and shine to candles, and convey a regal touch.

What to do with those cute but chunky clip-on earrings from the 1950s? Here's a fun idea that you can change to match your outfit. Add a hinged clasp to a keychain. Open the clip on the back of an earring, slide it through the clasp, and snap the clip down around it. And just like that, you've got a beautiful new keychain!

A clip-on earring can easily become a one-of-a-kind keychain.

Thrift stores are brimming with cheap frames just waiting to be embellished. The one below was purchased at a Salvation Army store for $1, and I added this beautiful cameo to the top of it. Now it looks like a million bucks!

Jewelry can also give new life to an old frame.

Turn a tea light from simple to spectacular with a tulle ribbon and a glamorous brooch. Simply tie a bow around the glass and stick the pin through the center of the knot. Light the candle and you're ready for anything from a romantic evening to a bridal shower!

Let the beauty, sparkle, and whimsy of your brooches be the jewelry focal point of your fashion ensembles or dinner party . . . until you use them to embellish a *Jewelry for Your Table* napkin ring set!

Add a pop of glamour to your table by dressing up your tea lights with vintage jewelry.

03

Put *a* Ring *on* It

A Brief History of Napkin Rings

IT'S GOT A *nice ring* TO IT

*A*lthough,

through the years, I've improved my kitchen competence, I am by no means what anybody would call a "great cook." Before a date, I used to make the following speech to any guy who took me out to dinner, as a sort of preemptive strike:

Just so you know, I'm kind of a workaholic. I travel all the time and work six or seven days a week. I'll probably never get married or have kids. I hate house cleaning, doing laundry and I'm a lousy cook. If you're okay with that, we can go ahead and order dinner. If not, I totally understand.

I can't believe more guys didn't leave skid marks.

Table décor can make even a simple meal seem elegant.

If I did get more serious with someone and eventually attempt to make him dinner, I would try to mask my barely edible dishes using clever subterfuge: I would dress to the nines, light candles everywhere, and set a dynamite table using gorgeous china, linens, and crystal. It's amazing how fabulous a meal of macaroni and cheese can taste when surrounded with mermaid-themed ambiance!

Happily, my homemaking game has improved immensely and thankfully, I've picked up a few new skills in the kitchen over the years. I still prefer to let someone else do the cooking so the dinner not only looks good, but actually tastes good as well. Regardless of what I serve my guests to eat, they are guaranteed a delicious presentation. Those who know me get a kick out of my creative tablescapes, especially my embellished napkin rings. A great deal of patience is required when it comes to special occasions, because I like to set the formal dining room table for events a couple of weeks beforehand so everyone (especially me) can enjoy looking at it.

One of the themes of this book is connecting your projects to your personal history and heritage. Every Thanksgiving I use my Wedgwood Cornucopia china, crystal, and silverware to create a fancy Thanksgiving tablescape. Because of the design of the china and crystal, I used gold as the central tone to build a set of vintage brooch napkin rings that complement the formal aesthetic of the table settings. Every one of these brooches is incredibly ornate and dates back to the 1920s and '40s— one of them even belonged to my grandmother. These heirlooms once sat in my jewelry box collecting dust. Now, every time I use them, I am especially thankful for the creative, strong, and loving women in my family who once wore them.

My Thanksgiving tablescape includes bejeweled candles and napkin rings that echo the rich gold tones of my Wedgwood china.

Before we jump into how to create a *Jewelry for Your Table* napkin ring set, let's appreciate the history of this pretty and practical accessory.

Of course there wouldn't be napkin rings at all, if it weren't for the napkins themselves.

The first known method of wiping off one's hands during a meal goes back to the days of the Spartans. Small pieces of dough were placed around the table for guests to press their fingers into: kneading the dough would clean off food residue. Later this technique evolved a bit with the use of slices of bread. Can you imagine wiping off your hands like that?

Eventually, the Romans developed a more civilized approach to guard against sticky fingers . . . the cloth napkin! These pieces of fabric were called a *mappa* and because the Romans ate reclined on a couch, the mappa would protect both the eater and the furniture from food debris.

Guests would bring their own mappas to dinner, and after the meal, extra food would be collected in them and taken home, doggy-bag style.

I have had this pair of cherubs for years. I think they're perfect for an afternoon tea.

In the sixteenth century, it became commonplace for individual napkins to be used at each table setting, but it wasn't until the nineteenth century that napkin rings (also called serviette rings) were added to the tables of the bourgeois class in France and soon became popular throughout the Western world. On the great transcontinental cruise liners, no table setting in the first-class compartment would be complete without a silver napkin ring engraved with the ship's emblem, and even the table number to which the passenger was assigned.

In America, napkin rings served a practical purpose: napkins weren't laundered daily, so each member of the family used a ring to identify his own personal napkin.

In her *Chicago Tribune* column, Anita Gold found this amusing anecdote about the practice of gathering napkins with rings for days, even weeks at a time:

The HOUSEWIFE'S LIBRARY, *printed in 1883, thought it was a disgusting habit and said that "unless the washing would thereby become crushingly heavy, the better way is to wash every napkin after one using. Dispense with the napkin ring."*

Traditionally, silver napkin rings engraved with the passenger's table number were part of the first-class service on transcontinental ocean liners.

Thankfully, homemakers throughout the Victorian era refused to give up these pretty dining accessories and eventually, with the advent of washing machines, the concern about hygiene was greatly diminished. Clean napkins for everybody, every day. Hallelujah!

Today, napkin rings serve as a design element for table settings and are sold individually, or in sets of two, four, or eight. They're primarily made of metal, silver or silver plate, wood, porcelain, glass, crystal, acrylic, or plastic and serve as an embellishment to a table setting. Much more than just a way to gather a napkin, these rings are a symbol of our love . . . for entertaining!

I found this colorful cloisonne napkin ring at an antique store. Savvy collectors can find them at reasonable prices.

Following page
Napkin rings can be found in a variety of styles as diverse as the jewelry you'll use to embellish them.

04
TREASURE HUNT

Gather Your Gems

Everything *old becomes new* AGAIN

Grandma and Grandpa Guerrero had a big, kind of creepy basement under their house in Chicago. When I was a kid, my brother, our cousins, and I would visit every summer and eventually end up playing down there, among boxes, extra furniture, and the rattle of their old washer and dryer. Although I was told not to, I loved to rummage through those boxes on the hunt for hidden treasures.

Treasure hunting for old jewelry began as child's play in my grandparents' basement.

Eventually, I would emerge upstairs, covered in dust, cobwebs, and strands upon strands of Grandma's costume jewelry necklaces. Sneaking into her bedroom, I'd spray on an obnoxious amount of perfume and head to Grandma's closet to dig around for scarves or a hat to complete my "look." Of course, I'd spend the rest of the day avoiding her (or at least until the copious amount of perfume wore off). Meanwhile, I would prowl around the house draping the necklaces around the side table

lampshades and using them to tie back the living room curtains. Très chic!

I've always loved discovering interesting, unused items (like damaged jewelry, shells from a vacation, and pieces of broken stained glass) and repurposing them into something glamorous, whimsical, or functional. The napkin rings I've embellished in *Jewelry for Your Table* are a perfect example of my passion for finding hidden treasures and putting them to good use.

In fact, this quote from Napoleon Bonaparte is one of my favorites: "Riches do not consist in the possession of treasures, but in the use made of them."

Before you can create a set of four napkin rings, you will need to compile the components of the project. The first and most important step is collecting the brooches that you'll be using for your set. Finding four coordinating pieces is both a challenge and an adventure.

To me, this is the fun part!

I want to help you develop your own unique design aesthetic while searching through flea markets, thrift stores, online, or in your own jewelry box to find pieces that will appeal to your personal style as well as your pocketbook. Here's what to ask yourself:

Question One:
What are you looking for?

One set of four *Jewelry for Your Table* napkin rings will require four brooches or pendants approximately one-and-a-half to two-and-a-half inches in diameter. Just make sure that the four pieces you choose are similar in size.

Another thing to consider when putting your set together is that all four brooches should have the same theme. (Check out Chapter Ten to see some of my favorite collections for inspiration.) Styles of pins vary greatly, so look for pieces that work in harmony together by color, era, shape, etc.

Some easy brooch and pendant collections to compile include flowers, butterflies, cameos, and rhinestone/pearl combinations. Cross pendants are plentiful, too. Go with your gut and pick a collection of four pieces that appeals to you.

Question Two:
Where are you looking?

Chances are, you won't find all four of your treasures in one place, and that's the beauty of it. The pieces aren't supposed to be identical. You want them to be slightly different, yet harmonious . . . as if you've collected them over time. This helps the project look handcrafted rather than mass produced.

Shop your own closet first. The least expensive and most personal pieces are the ones you already own, know, and love. Dust off your favorites and start with these. Then call your mom, sisters, aunts, and grandmothers to get permission to raid their jewelry boxes, too. Using costume jewelry

the counter or in the back of the shop. These bags are sometimes full of damaged or scratched pieces, but because you will break the pin off the back later and want them to look "vintage" anyway, this can be a perfect and inexpensive way to buy many brooches at once.

Another good resource for finding pins and pendants are craft stores carrying jewelry supplies. Although these pieces aren't old, many are made to look vintage and can add to your collection without breaking the bank.

As a last resort, to fill in a set, consider going online. I had a collection of three ballerina pins in various shades of pink enamel and rhinestones, but I couldn't find a fourth in the thrift stores or flea markets to complete it. I wanted to make a set of *Jewelry for Your Table* napkin rings for a friend's baby shower and found the perfect pink "tiny dancer" on eBay to finish the collection in time for the party. Going online to find pins is really convenient (simply do a Google search for, say, "ballerina pins" or "costume jewelry pins," and you'll see what I mean). Plus, they deliver to your door. You will, however, pay for that convenience and half the fun, for me at least, is finding my little gems in person.

Question Three:
How much should you spend?

Cost will be a factor for most of us when collecting our brooches and only you can determine what your budget will allow. Because I make so many sets, my formula is this: I try to keep the average cost of a set of four brooches to about $50, so each pin should be around $12–$13. Of course some pins are pricier, and others I get in "bulk

that's already "in the family" means there's an instant emotional connection to the project. Don't tell them what you're going to do with their old brooches or pendants because you may want to create a set for them as a gift.

Scour thrift stores next. The Salvation Army is my personal favorite because the money spent there goes back into your community to support much needed social services like their adult rehabilitation centers and other programs for the needy. Many independent thrift stores also help support local charities. Tell the manager what you're looking for and leave a contact number with her so she can call you when a new batch of costume jewelry comes in. Be friendly and accessible. If she knows you'll potentially be a regular customer, she'll give you a heads up when new pieces arrive so you can have first crack at the jewelry before it gets picked over.

I love shopping at flea markets, garage sales, antique stores, and consignment shops. Make sure to ask if they have "bulk bags" of costume jewelry behind bags" much cheaper, so I do a bit of creative math to get there. Remember, you'll also need to buy the other supplies for the project like adhesive and napkin rings, so you will need to keep the cost of the brooches as reasonably priced as possible. Paying with cash rather than credit helps. It will keep you on budget and vendors will often knock down the price or allow you to barter with them.

When buying costume jewelry from flea market vendors, don't be afraid to negotiate. That's right . . . we Americans don't use this skill very much because in most chain stores the prices are set by a corporate office. But at flea markets, thrift shops, and antique stores they often need to get rid of a large quantity of items quickly to make a profit, so they may be willing to negotiate. I always try to get a discount first. You'd be surprised what a smile and a simple remark can do to save you money! I usually lead with, "Is today a half-off sale?" Before long you'll be bartering like a pro.

Be sure to bring along a magnifying glass, craft goggles, or reading glasses to look for flaws—especially on the backside with the clasp or pin. You will eventually be breaking this part off anyway so you can get a real bargain if you point out that it's damaged. Also look carefully for missing stones or beads. You can still buy and repair it with beads from a craft store, but if it's broken you shouldn't pay full price.

So to save the most money and find the best emotional connection to your jewelry, look for the pieces in this order: shop your closet first, then find pieces from family members and friends. Next, try thrift shops and garage sales. Then hit flea markets, consignment stores, and antique shops. Finally, fill in your set by shopping online or in craft stores.

Now that you've begun to find gorgeous pins and pendants for your *Jewelry for Your Table* napkin rings, it's time to "set up shop" at home as your collection grows.

When not wearing my pins, I roll around in them. (Just kidding! One could get pricked doing that.)

05

CURATING YOUR COLLECTION

Organization Is Everything

From *messy* to *dressy*

When

I first began collecting brooches, I would throw them in bags, trinket boxes, kitchen drawers, my bathroom vanity, and, at one time, even into a big wooden box that I inexplicably kept in my oven. This reveals two things: 1.) That I did very little cooking 2.) Why I was single for so long.

> Some people think organizing is a chore, but for me, organizing jewelry is a blast.

Because I was working hard at my "day job" as a sports reporter and living in my first house—a tiny one bedroom Spanish bungalow in the Hollywood Hills—I had very little time and even less room to organize my collection. Like a chipmunk hoarding nuts in a burrow for the future, I was squirreling away my brooches all over my home for future art projects. At one point I was so confused about what I had that I pulled out every pin from its secret lair and laid them out all over the place—on every table top, kitchen counter, my bed, and even my floors. A girlfriend came over and announced that it looked like a jewelry box had thrown up all over my house.

No bueno.

In addition to the clutter, I discovered that by tossing my pieces of costume jewelry on top of each other in bags or into shoe boxes, I was damaging them. Some of the rhinestones had popped out and beads or pearls were scattered at the bottom of bags and drawers. I had no way of knowing where these broken pieces had come from. Word to the wise . . . as your collection of brooches grows, and it will rapidly, it's important to keep them clean, protected, and organized from the very beginning. Had I done that twenty years ago it would've saved a ton of headaches (and dozens of pins) later on!

I inspect and clean each piece when I bring it home and then sort.

DIVIDE *by* THEME

If your collection is inspired by pin styles or motifs (animals, crowns, cameos, etc.) then separate them into groups of like design.

DIVIDE *by* COLOR

Some people will prefer to create their napkin ring projects based on the color composition of the jewelry. If so, that's an easy and beautiful way to organize your collection.

DIVIDE *by* ERA

Check out the list of which brooches were popular through the years in Chapter Two and organize your jewelry by era (Victorian, art deco, mod, new wave, etc.)

DIVIDE *by* PERSONAL CONNECTION

(This one's my favorite.) If you have pieces from your mother, aunts, grandmothers, etc., keep these together and label them. Nothing is more special than creating a set of *Jewelry for Your Table* napkin rings made from your own family heirlooms!

When you bring your jewelry home from the flea market, antique store, or simply downstairs from the attic, put a clean dish towel or tablecloth over a counter or table in a well lit area of your house. Carefully remove your jewelry from its package and place it on the cloth. Use your magnifying glass or goggles to inspect the front and back of the pin. Did a piece of crystal pop off in transit? Don't throw away the package or bag it came in before you check. If any pieces have fallen off, simply glue them back on with a jewelry adhesive. You can find many options at craft stores.

Next, you'll want to gently dust off and clean the brooch with a soft cloth (I use small pieces of old t-shirts). If you detect that the pin has tarnished over time, you can dip a Q-tip in a cleaning solution (read the instructions carefully) and wipe it off.

When every brooch has been cleaned and repaired, lay them all out together and consider them carefully. At this point you should decide how to organize them. Although it sounds simple, it's actually trickier than you'd suspect. There are several ways to catalog your treasure trove of brooches. To the left are a few suggestions.

Once you've organized your pins and pendants into groups, you'll need to store them safely so you can wear and enjoy them until ultimately embellishing your napkin rings with them. Decide whether you have room to stack plastic boxes in shelves and drawers or if you'd prefer to hang the collections on a rack or in a closet.

I recommend a trip to a home goods or arts and crafts store to pick up the following:

Hanging jewelry organizer bags (this is the easiest system, in my opinion)

Plastic, multi-compartment, bead organizer boxes

Felt

Label maker or stickers and pens

Tiny Ziploc bead baggies

Plastic bead organizer boxes are perfect for storing your costume jewelry in drawers or shelves. They can usually be found with various sized compartments to fit your brooches. Because they are sturdy, you can stack them on top of each other to keep the pieces safe.

I like to cut the felt into small squares to line each compartment. This keeps the jewelry from sliding around and adds a cushion of protection beneath the pin.

Next, I label both the top and front panels of the organizer boxes with the name of the collection and a description of the contents. For example: "Crown Jewels,"

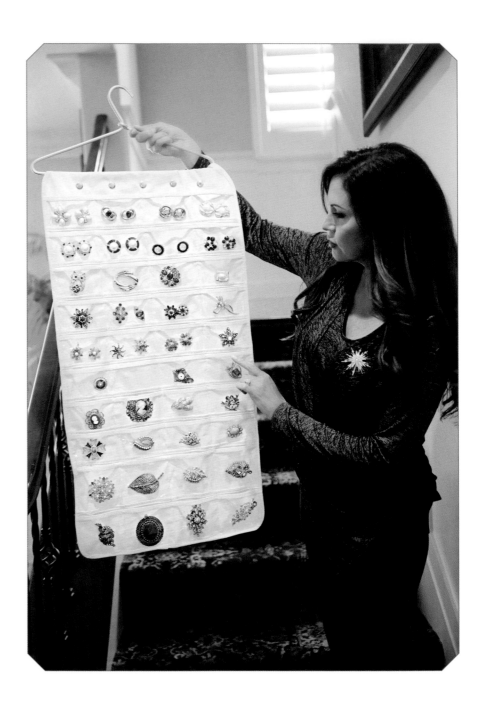

"Cameo Appearance," "Medieval Medallions," "Blue Rhinestones," "Art Deco," "Family Brooches," etc.

I use the tiny plastic bags to keep loose rhinestones or beads together with the brooch they belong to until I can get around to repairing them. This is also a great way to keep pairs of earrings together.

Finally, find a cupboard or a set of shelves inside your home to store the plastic organizers containing your collection. Avoid putting them in your garage, attic, or basement, which may not be weatherproofed. Extreme heat or cold can damage your jewelry. Once you've organized your pins, it becomes easier to pick the sets of brooches you will transform into *Jewelry for Your Table*.

06

THE PERFECT RING
for YOUR BLING

Create a Great Match with
Color, Texture, and Shape

A VERY *complimentary* COMBINATION

Just like the brooch itself, *Jewelry for Your Table* napkin rings are gorgeous from the front and functional from behind. Kind of like the opposite of the '90s era mullet: "business in the front, party in the back."

Your napkin rings will be pretty from the front and practical from behind.

With this project, the jewelry is the star of the show once the table is set and the candles are lit. But without it being anchored from behind to the right napkin ring, you might as well pin it to your blouse then dump it in your jewelry box after dinner, rarely to be seen again for months or even years.

I love to display my napkin rings in a crystal bowl that reflects their sparkle!

Creating a *Jewelry for Your Table* napkin ring set will ensure that you will enjoy the beauty of your brooches every time you entertain guests, sit down for Sunday supper, or invite friends over for a home-cooked meal. Even when I don't have my table set, I leave some of my jewelry-embellished napkin rings out in a crystal bowl on a countertop or a coffee table. Sometimes I leave my formal dining room table set for days to show off my napkin rings. They're a gorgeous home décor focal point, sparkle in any light, and are a great conversation piece.

Once you've selected the brooches you'll use for this project, the next step is to decide what kind of ring you'll be attaching each brooch to. The most common rings you'll see are made of metal, wood, or plastic. I prefer metal for most of my sets because the shine complements the jewelry and metal rings are sturdier than plastic, but there are some exceptions, which I'll detail shortly.

In keeping with my concept of creating a project that has a personal connection to you or your family, the first place I suggest you look for rings to attach your

jewelry to is at home. Bring the brooches or pendants you've selected over to your kitchen drawers or dining room hutch to see if you already own a set of rings that will complement them. If your jewelry is gold toned, find plain gold toned napkin rings. If your jewelry is silver, find silver rings.

Within the metal category, these three tones will complement most of your brooches or pendants: silver, gold, and bronze. Turn over your jewelry to examine the back and choose a metallic tone that coordinates with it.

Another beautiful, earthy option is wood. These types of rings are usually thicker and chunkier than metallic rings and look amazing with '70s-era costume jewelry like owls, ethnic beaded pendants, and safari-inspired pieces. Wooden rings also add richness and texture to rustic-looking floral brooches from the '30s and '40s.

While metal rings look beautiful with sparkling gems, woods and plastics can also create dramatic presentations when paired with the right brooch styles.

I mentioned that some of the napkin rings you'll see are made of plastic or acrylic. Although I would never pair this type of ring with, say, art deco brooches, they are absolutely perfect when embellished with '60s-era mod "flower power" pins in those groovy citrus shades that were once so popular (remember avocado-colored refrigerators?) and are making a strong

comeback today in hip, mid-century modern–inspired homes. Clear acrylic rings work well here, as do solids like white, yellow, and even black for a dramatic flair. Plastic rings also look great with neon-colored pins from the '80s.

> Some carefully selected rings and a few other tricks will give you the option of keeping the backs on your brooches.

Finally, I'm going to suggest a way to "fudge" on this project a little bit, especially if you are uneasy about breaking the back of pins that have been in your family for generations: find beaded, cloth, wire, woven, or burlap-covered napkin rings. The soft surface makes it easy to pin your brooch directly onto the ring so you never have to damage a family heirloom, but you still get the same *Jewelry for Your Table* look. Another way to "cheat" is to wrap a length of ribbon around a metal napkin ring, secure the ends in a knot and pin the brooch through the knot. Easy and beautiful!

What about the shape? Although most of the rings that I use are round because they are more common, oval or square rings will work too. Remember that a napkin will be stuffed, rolled, or folded into the ring, so the fabric will keep the brooch stable on the top of the project even if the napkin ring itself is round.

The only shape that doesn't work for our project is if the outside of the ring is extremely curved. We are going to glue the jewelry to the outside top of the ring, so if the surface is too rounded, the adhesive won't have a solid surface to stick to.

Finally, where (outside of your home) are you going to find all of these plain napkin rings to embellish? You'd be surprised how cheap and easy they are to gather. My dad regularly scours garage sales—his early morning weekend hobby since I was a kid—and he's constantly finding sets of metallic napkin rings for a couple of bucks. They are usually stored in bins near the dishware section of thrift shops, and large home goods chain stores sell huge varieties of them, too. (Always check the sale rack first.)

When you get them home, clean the rings, separate them by style or color, and store them in tissue paper, packed into small containers (I use shoe boxes) to keep them organized until you're ready to embellish them.

07

LET'S GET PREPPED!

Your Supplies and Workspace

TOOLS OF THE TRADE:
FROM ALL THAT
glitters to glue

Besides

being a sentimental fool (see Chapter One), I am also easily distracted. Not unlike an eight-year-old left to her own devices in a toy shop, if I am set loose in an arts and crafts store without a shopping list, I will wander every aisle playing with all the "goodies" until the manager turns off the lights or someone calls the police to order an APB to track me down at the far reaches of the store, covered in glue, glitter, stickers, and a smile.

"Hi, Officer . . . is it really midnight? I had no idea. But check out this foam wreath I hope to cover with these peacock feathers, rhinestones, and royal blue tulle!"

(Actually, that sounds amazing.)

Point being, if I head to a craft store without a plan, I am doomed. This quote by Alexander Graham Bell sums it up thusly:

"Before anything else, preparation is the key to success."

So far you've laid the groundwork to assemble a *Jewelry for Your Table* napkin ring set by selecting the main components of the project: the brooches or pendants and the coordinating napkin rings.

Now it's time for a trip to the arts and crafts store, armed with a shopping list of the following supplies:

Magnifying, Hands-Free Goggles, Glasses, *or* Visor

This item is optional, but fair warning: you will be working with small pieces of jewelry and carefully looking for at least two places on the back of each pin to attach the ring. Some kind of magnifying glass will be incredibly helpful, especially if you are (like me) over thirty and have a hard time reading small print. There is no shame in wearing goofy-looking goggles. Just remove them before taking a selfie.

Metal-to-Metal *or* Jewelry Adhesive

Usually a clear, silicone glue works best, but read the label carefully, keeping in mind the materials you will be using. Are you attaching your brooches to metal rings, wood rings, or plastic rings? E6000 works well for most of my projects.

Jewelry Pliers

You will be using this small tool to pry the pin gently off of the back of the jewelry. There are several styles you can choose from. Select one that has ridges or grooves on the inside to help grasp the pin securely.

Jewelry Tweezers *and a* Crayon

I use these to carefully pick up and hold a small bead or rhinestone when I repair or replace pieces that have popped off the front of a brooch. Believe it or not, a crayon can do the same task. Gently press a crayon to the front of a gem (it will stick—like magic!), dip the back in glue, and attach it to your brooch.

Wooden Sticks

Grab a bag of these small wooden sticks with a flat end (rather than toothpick style). These are great tools to help wipe off excess glue from your project.

Two Dozen Corks

If you are like me and enjoy a glass of wine in the evening, you probably collect corks. If not, you can find them at a craft store or check with a local wine bar to arrange setting some aside for you. These are for your "cork box" to lay out your sets while they dry overnight.

Cardboard Gift Box

This is the other component you'll need for the cork box. The best size is about 9 by 12 inches. If you are planning to do a large group of napkin rings at once, you can use the box lid as well.

White *or* Craft Glue

You'll use this kind of adhesive to attach your corks to the inside of the box. I prefer Weldbond, but you can use your favorite glue for this task.

Paper Towels

No matter how careful you are, glue will be dripping from the pieces themselves or from your wood sticks. Always have a paper towel ready.

Jewelry Box Tray Inserts

This is an alternative to building a cork box. A felt-covered jewelry box tray insert can hold the rings in place while the glue dries.

An Empty Wine Bottle

This will be where you'll deposit the pins you break off the back of your brooches. Of course, for safety reasons, you can't throw the pins directly in the trash, so placing them in a wine bottle is a great solution. Enjoy emptying it first!

Once you bring home your supplies, consider where you want to set up your workspace. One of the great things about creating *Jewelry for Your Table* napkin rings is that you don't need a huge amount of space. Find a flat work area in a well lit room with plenty of ventilation. (The fumes from the glue can be pretty strong.)

Choose a well-lit workspace with a nice flat tabletop that you should protect with an old cloth or dishtowel.

In my house I work at a large, center island in my kitchen where I get lots of natural light and I can open an exterior door to let in fresh air.

Finally, lay down an old tablecloth or a large dish towel to protect your table or counter from glue and tiny particles of metal from the backs of the jewelry you'll be breaking.

Once you lay out your brooches, napkin rings, and the rest of your supplies, pull up a stool, roll up your sleeves, and let's get to work!

08

LET'S GET STARTED!

Step-by-Step Details

Pop a cork,
AND LET THE
fun BEGIN

*E*very

time I post a set of my *Jewelry for Your Table* napkin rings on social media I get hundreds of responses from people asking me to teach them how to make these treasures themselves. That is why I decided to write this book. Although the steps I use to physically create the pieces sound easy, the hardest part is pulling together the brooches and rings for your collection. I couldn't convey this in a simple Facebook post so I wanted to write a book detailing the entire process. Since you've made it all the way to Chapter Eight, congratulations! The most time-consuming element of the project is over.

In spite of this, don't let the fact that there are only a few steps in this chapter fool you. Because every brooch or pendant is different, you will have the unique challenge of breaking each pin off the back and attaching it to its napkin ring base. What I will share here is the basic process, step-by-step, for creating your set of *Jewelry for Your Table* napkin rings.

Make Your Cork Box

This is the device you'll need to set your embellished napkin rings into so they can dry overnight. The reason I use corks is that they "grip" the smooth rings securely to hold them in place without moving or slipping. Obviously, you'll need to create this first so that when you've attached the brooch you can immediately set and balance the ring in the box between corks to dry safely.

A cork box will ensure that your embellished rings set securely overnight.

Begin by running a line of craft glue on the inside bottom of a box about a quarter of an inch from the horizontal edge. Then lay a row of corks along this line, resting against the inside edge of the box.

Lay down another line of craft glue about one and one-quarter to one and one-half inches from your first row of corks and then lay your second line of corks on top of the glue. Repeat this until you reach the far end of the box. Let dry.

Step Two:
Examine and Repair

Using your magnifying goggles, carefully inspect the front
of your brooch or pendant for missing rhinestones, dirt,
or tarnish stains. Repair these issues now. Once you attach
the jewelry to the napkin ring it will be harder to clean
or fix. Most craft stores carry extra crystals, beads, and
pearls in a variety of colors and sizes. I always have a
sizeable selection on hand for quick repairs. Use a Q-tip
dipped in jewelry cleaner if the brooch needs it. Be sure
to read the directions to see if the type of metal or stones
in your jewelry are compatible with the product. In the
past I have taken two broken pieces of jewelry and combined
them together to make one intact brooch.

> Now is the time to make sure your jewelry is clean
> and flaw-free.

Turn the brooch over and examine how the pin is attached. Because you will be gluing it to the napkin ring, you need to remove the straight pin and possibly the entire device behind the brooch.

Using your jewelry pliers, carefully grip the straight pin near the base, close to where it attaches to the brooch. Gently rock the pin back and forth until either the pin itself breaks off, or the entire fastening device peels away from the jewelry.

Carefully discard the straight pin—I usually toss mine in an empty wine bottle or a jar, and after completing an entire set, I seal up the container and throw it away.

Once the pin is removed, dust off any metal particles from the back of the jewelry. Don't worry if some of the brooches have the fastening device removed or just the straight pin. Remember, every piece of jewelry is different and unique. They don't all have to match, especially on the back where they will be attached to the napkin rings.

Removing the hardware using jewelry pliers may mean simply removing the pin (right) or the whole fastening device (opposite, near). Then dispose of the pin in a safe place, such as an empty wine bottle (opposite, far).

Step Four:
Glue the Brooch to the Napkin Ring

Before opening your glue or adhesive, look at the area behind the brooch to see where the jewelry will touch the napkin ring. Each brooch should attach in at least two places, preferably three, to get the most secure grip.

Either A) squeeze the adhesive onto those points on the brooch or B) add the adhesive directly onto the ring. C) Carefully press the jewelry and napkin ring together. D) Using your wooden stick, wipe off the excess glue and deposit on a paper towel. (See images A–D, beginning opposite.)

Before gluing, find the two or three contact points where the brooch will touch the ring. Then either put the adhesive on the brooch, or directly on the ring at those points. Carefully press jewelry to ring. Wipe off excess glue. Let set and dry. The next day, remove any excess dried glue.

After holding it for a few minutes to let the adhesive begin to set, place the ring carefully between the rows of your cork box making sure the jewelry is centered on the napkin ring by looking at it from directly above. Leave to dry overnight. In the morning, carefully pull off any errant strings or drips of dried glue.

A final thought here about your finished ring . . . when it's dry and you can pick it up and turn it over, don't worry that you may be able to see the back of the brooch or the clasp from underneath. I believe that these details make the project look more "vintage" and authentic (See image E, below). The pieces are literally *Jewelry for Your Table*, so your guests will be delighted to see the way you've hand-crafted real brooches onto the rings. If I can break off the straight pin and save the clasp, I think it makes the finished piece more textured and interesting.

 09

"Framing" *with a*
Fabulous Napkin

Tips for Terrific Tablescapes

PULLING
it all
TOGETHER

I like to think of *Jewelry for Your Table* napkin rings as tiny little works of art, but what would a masterpiece be without the perfect frame?

To me, a cloth napkin works like a frame by using color, shape, and texture to enhance the ring, to complement the jewelry, and to pull together the separate pieces of your set into one coordinated theme.

When viewed by themselves, the jewelry-embellished napkin rings are beautiful, individual items that placed together on a table convey a similar motif. Once they are displayed with matching napkins, the set has a cohesion and richness that brings the design of the project to life.

Adding matching napkins to your individual napkin rings turns them into a high-impact cohesive set.

The perfect napkin actually serves several purposes: to frame or enhance the napkin rings, to pull together the separate rings into one coordinated set, and to complement the rest of the table setting. (Also, you can wipe your fingers on it.)

When I gift a set of *Jewelry for Your Table* napkin rings, I always include a set of quality linen, silk, or cotton napkins as part of the "presentation." Pretty and practical! Better yet, if you can sew, whip up a set. Absolutely nothing is more thoughtful than a hand-crafted present! Later in the book I'll share some other creative ideas for gifting these sets.

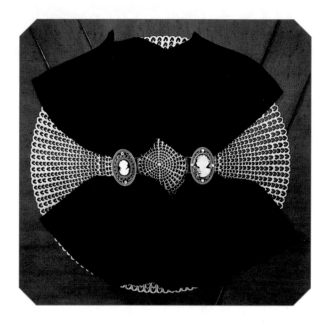

While on the subject of napkins, keep in mind that you don't have to spend a fortune. Just as these brooches are vintage, you may want to shop thrift stores and flea markets for vintage napkins as well.

The kind of napkin you select can really set the tone for the rings. For example, a deep, midnight blue, silk napkin in a rhinestone art deco napkin ring conveys glamour and formality while a beige, rough-edged, burlap napkin in a vintage, floral napkin ring looks rustic and evokes a shabby chic aesthetic. I love the romance of coordinating an ivory, embroidered napkin tucked into a "Lovers' Locket" style napkin ring or the drama of a gold, satin napkin in a napkin ring embellished with a Gothic cross.

While picking out a napkin, don't be afraid of patterns! Gingham napkins look beautiful with enamel, floral brooch embellished rings, and a bold, batik print napkin is amazing tucked into a wooden ring embellished with '70s-era, earthy, ethnic pendants.

Don't be afraid of bold patterns. They can enhance, rather than detract from, your napkin rings.

If I'm setting a particularly fancy table for an event or a holiday, I sometimes use two "napkins" in the ring: one of cloth to use on the lap and another made of tulle or lace to add a layer of texture and glamour to the place setting. Another fun idea is to tuck a peacock feather behind the napkin and into the ring once you've set the table. Or just a single flower—I love using white roses!

The same set of embellished napkin rings can look completely different simply by changing up the napkins you tuck into them. A baby-blue rhinestone collection looks fresh and crisp with starched, white napkins and would be perfect for a baby shower luncheon, but when paired with black or midnight blue napkins, that same set evokes a dressy elegance, perfect for a formal dinner party.

Experiment to see how your rings look different with various colors and styles of napkins.

The way you fold, stuff or roll a napkin into the *Jewelry for Your Table* napkin rings makes a huge difference in the look of your table.

As a general rule, folding the napkin looks more traditionally classic, rolling the fabric feels a bit more casual or romantic, and stuffing the napkin through the ring gives a more organic and natural appearance to the place setting.

> The way the napkin is folded or rolled enhances the overall effect.

If you are throwing a large dinner party, don't forget that the napkins can pull together different sets or styles of napkin rings. For example, I use my eight piece "Cameo Appearance" collection with eight of my "Gothic Crosses" to set a big event table. I stagger the rings in both of the sets for every other guest and pull the whole look together using burgundy linen napkins. It is gorgeous!

The takeaway from this chapter is to think of the embellished napkin rings as the "super star" of the place setting, and the perfect napkin as the essential "supporting actor" that lets your *Jewelry for Your Table* collection really shine!

10

MY FAVORITE COLLECTIONS

Inspiration and Ideas

THESE ARE A FEW OF MY *favorite things*

**emember**

when you were a kid and demanded of your mom while side-eying your siblings, "Which one of us do you love the best?" If your mom was anything like mine, she'd smile, wink and say, "Don't be silly, honey. I love each of you the same!" A perfectly diplomatic answer but I'm pretty sure I drove her up the wall while my much sweeter brother was far more lovable.

After making hundreds of vintage jewelry embellished napkin rings, a girlfriend asked me which one was my favorite, and while I was considering the sets I wanted to feature in this book, it's been hard to decide on the ones I like best . . . I love them all!

The following *Jewelry for Your Table* napkin ring sets were the most meaningful to me for a variety of reasons. I hope you too will find them special and inspiring.

Because this set was my first and includes a brooch from my grandmother (a red poinsettia), I think this will always be my favorite. The rings look perfect with my Lenox Christmas china, and I currently have twenty-four pieces in this collection.

Art Deco

To me, this is my most glamorous set. The rhinestones and pearls lend sparkle and shine to a candlelit table, and they look fantastic with any color napkin. So far I have eight pieces in this set with eight brooches in storage for future projects.

107

Men's Club

Just because *Jewelry for Your Table* encourages you to use vintage brooches and pendants, it doesn't mean the end result is always "girly" or feminine looking. This collection features masculine pieces like the lion pendant and the swordfish pin. This set has gold accents, and I have another in silver.

Cameo Appearance

Every time I post one of these pieces on social media, women love them! I began this collection with one cameo from each of my grandmothers, so I have a real emotional connection to these. I now have three sets of cameo napkin rings with different color combinations.

Safari Wood

My safari collections are charming and work with both metal rings and the wooden ones you see here. They look earthy and have a little bit of a '70s-era ethnic vibe. One of these sets is all owls, which for some reason was a popular style of brooch in the late '60s through the late '70s.

Gothic Crosses

This collection is both dramatic and striking when paired with the right napkins. I prefer them with gold, bronze, or ivory. It's also pretty easy to find lots of crucifix pendants in a nice size for this project. This set looks wonderful in either a Mediterranean or Spanish style home, like mine.

Vintage Swedish

My friend and *Inside Edition* colleague Deborah Norville married a man from Sweden. As a gift, I collected vintage pewter Swedish brooches from the mid-twentieth century, all with an origin stamp on the back. I paired them with napkins that were true to a clean mid-century style, creating an homage to her family's heritage.

Medieval Medallions

Here's another striking look for a dressier tablescape. I adore the richness of the jewel tones and these add a lot of texture and shine to a place setting. They also have a fantastic, regal aesthetic.

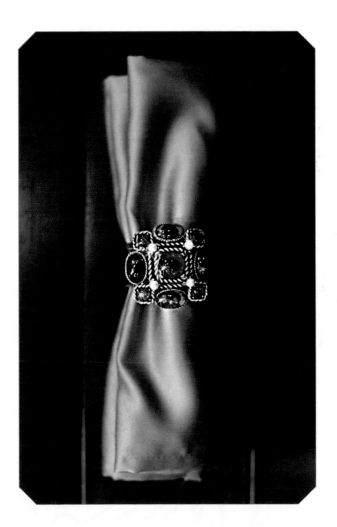

Emerald City

These green gems with rhinestones and pearls add instant elegance to the table! A lot of china patterns incorporate green with gold trim so these are easy to coordinate with vintage plates and can also be used to glam up a holiday table.

Chasing the Sun

I'm a passionate traveler and have collected several sunburst pins from various corners of the earth, including Italy and Chile. My friend Priscilla also found a couple of these at an antique store in Arizona. This sunny collection always puts a smile on my face.

Blush Bouquet

How sweet are these? I am drawn to very romantic vintage jewelry and these brooches in shades of baby blue and pink coordinated well together. I love this look with an ivory napkin and china found at a thrift store.

Victorian Gold

This is a beautiful, romantic set and fun to curate because there are lots of designs that can be used: flowers, cameos, angels, hearts, etc. If it looks like it came out of your great-grandmother's jewelry box, it would probably work in this collection. You can continue the theme with vintage ivory napkins or go for broke and use a lace design.

Painted Lovers

This is one of the richest looking sets I've created. The lovers painted on these gorgeous brooches were very popular in the last century but can still be found in flea markets and antique marts. They tend to be a little more expensive ($15-$50 a piece), but the result is gorgeous!

Pretty in Pink

I'm a sucker for the femininity of this collection. It started with a floral pin a girlfriend gave me years ago, and it's my go-to set when I have a ladies' lunch. They look fresh with white or silver napkins, but if you use black napkins instead, the sex appeal is off the charts! *Lingerie for Your Table?* Hmmmm . . .

Lovers' Lockets

This is a set I make for newlyweds so I create just two per collection. Almost everyone has had a locket, and of course the charm is opening it up and finding an image of your true love. This is an intimate way to personalize a table setting by using wedding photos.

Of course, because all of these sets are one of a kind, you won't to be able to "copy" these collections exactly, but I encourage you to use them as inspiration to create the projects that best reflect the design aesthetic that appeals to you!

11

PARTY ON *and* PASS ON THIS CRAFT

Gifts and Gatherings

FROM PAST *to* PRESENTS

*f* your girlfriends are anything like mine, prepare yourself. The first time you throw a dinner party using your newly created *Jewelry for Your Table* napkin rings they will: A) Freak out and exclaim, "Oh my goodness! These are amazing! I love them!"; and then B) Demand to know how you made them, followed by an offer to buy your set and when you say, "Heck, no," they will beg you to teach them how you did it.

At this juncture you will have three options:

1.

Politely decline by explaining that you're planning to make her a set for her birthday.

2.

Buy her a copy of Jewelry for Your Table *so she can learn how to make her own.*

3.

Throw a Jewelry for Your Table *party and invite the ladies in your life over for a glass of champagne and a tutorial on how to create their own sets of jewelry-embellished napkin rings. (A really incredible hostess would provide a copy of* Jewelry for Your Table *in the gift bag at the end of the night. I'm just saying.)*

Invite friends over for a *Jewelry for Your Table* party where they can learn the technique, trade brooches, and go home with a wonderful keepsake or an incredible gift for someone special.

I have thrown several of these soirees, and they are incredibly fun and a wonderful way to share this project with friends and family while encouraging their creative instincts. I know women who aren't "crafters" and are completely intimidated by the thought of picking up a paintbrush, a glass cutter, or knitting needles, but all of them love jewelry and setting a pretty table, so this is an activity that will appeal to them, has only a few steps, and will allow your friends to go home with a gorgeous, handcrafted project that they can be proud of and use every day.

It's also a party that is fairly simple to prepare for. Here are a few, easy tips:

Pick a casual daytime "Garden Party" theme or a dressier "Girls' Night In."

Give your guests at least two weeks' notice.

Invite just 2–6 people. Any more makes it difficult to personally instruct everybody; chaos will ensue and glue will be everywhere.

Ask your friends to bring brooches or pendants from their own jewelry boxes, some to keep for their own set, and others to "trade" with fellow guests. This part is really fun! You can choose a "theme" for example: ask them to bring Christmas pins, floral brooches, or pick a color scheme.

I taught my friend Deena, and my stepmom Pam, how to make *Jewery for Your Table* sets during a garden party.

Have several brooches to contribute to your guest's collections. They don't have to make four or six pieces. A set of two is fine.

I also like to provide pretty, ivory cloth napkins for everybody so they can go home with "frames" for their works of art.

Set a table with a plastic tablecloth or plastic placemats for each guest and provide all the supplies they'll need (glue, napkin rings, pliers, wooden sticks, etc.) Remind them to bring reading glasses, if needed.

Scatter "cork boxes" or jewelry box inserts around the table for everyone to set their rings on to dry, as well as empty wine bottles or jars where they can discard their broken straight pins.

Provide mini cork boxes or jewelry holders for guests to take their sets home in following the party. Remind them to let the collection dry for twenty-four hours.

I love sharing this craft with others and the best part, without a doubt, is giving these sets as gifts.

I think the best way to present them is in sets of four with coordinating napkins in a gift box, basket, or tray that enhances the design of the collection.

This beautiful gift presentation includes four rings with coordinating napkins in a lovely box. A mirror on the inside lid helps bring in light to make the creations sparkle.

Because the brooch itself is the focal point of the craft, a pretty way to present it is in a jewelry box. I prefer the ones that are vintage or look like they could be: wooden, fabric covered, or embellished.

If the set you're gifting has an art deco theme, think about arranging them on a mirrored tray with a black satin bow. I have a gorgeous collection called "Golden Pearl" that looks spectacular on a mother of pearl serving tray I found on sale at a home goods store for twelve dollars. All of the brooches feature mother of pearl details.

Let your imagination run wild when considering how to gift your *Jewelry for Your Table* sets. Almost any kind of a box or basket could work, depending on the theme, so begin to save interesting containers now.

For many years my friend Stephanie and her mother, Jeanne, had been gifting each other snail collectibles. They believe snails bring good luck, and Stephanie's home has whimsical examples of this cute little creature everywhere, including her garden. After Jeanne passed away, I began collecting rhinestone snail brooches to embellish a set of napkin rings as a Christmas gift for Stephanie. A few years ago, she had her kitchen area remodeled with striking stainless-steel appliances and black granite so I thought these cute silver and black snails with black napkins would look amazing on her dining room table to complement the new décor. I presented four of them to her in a sparkly red box and I intend to gift her two more for each upcoming holiday to expand her collection.

A romantic way to present a pair of "Lovers' Lockets" napkin rings for a wedding or shower gift is to tuck them into a champagne box. (Ask a local restaurant or wine bar to save them for you.) If you really want to add a personal touch, have the cloth napkins you're presenting embroidered with the couple's initials. And don't forget to put their photos in the lockets!

Presenting a pair of "Lovers' Lockets" napkin rings in a repurposed champagne box adds to the romantic gesture.

Earlier I mentioned that some of the sets I've created are masculine-looking rather than glitzy ("Men's Club," "Anchors Away," "King of the Jungle," "Military Medals"), so I've come up with a creative way to gift these for the men in your life. The most striking way to present them is in a wooden cigar box. For an extra touch of whimsy (and practicality so the rings don't knock into each other), put cigars in between the rings. The ultimate gift for the man who has everything.

For the man in your life, arrange the napkin rings in a wooden cigar box.

110

Baskets and pretty fabric boxes are some of the many other great options for gift presentations.

My go-to presentation for the collections is a simple, woven basket. Just about every set looks great like this, especially the ones with wooden rings, a rustic floral design, or medieval and Gothic themes. You can find many baskets of different styles and sizes in thrift stores. I have found them for as little as one dollar each at a local Salvation Army Thrift Store.

Most stationery stores or gift shops sell pretty vintage-looking paper covered boxes for storage or gifting purposes. You can also cover shoe boxes with patterned contact paper or fabric. I love the idea of gluing corks on the bottom of the box in between the rings to keep them from sliding around. The finished look is both homespun and charming.

Finally, a simple yet elegant way to gift a *Jewelry for Your Table* napkin ring is by itself, in a small fabric covered box. Kind of like a ring presentation, but your special gift box is for a one-of-a-kind "mini masterpiece."

I hope your takeaway from this book is to appreciate and enjoy the heirlooms in your life and to discover the magical pieces that were once an important part of someone else's, to discover a design aesthetic that you didn't know you had, and to pass along to family and friends the passion you've acquired for these vintage treasures. I hope this book inspires and blesses you. Writing it has blessed and inspired me.

Thank you
for joining me on this journey.

142